POPCORN

Prayer Journal

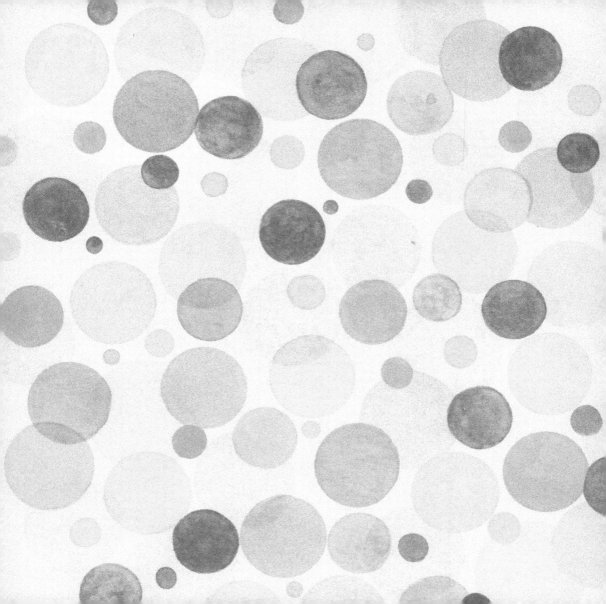

POPCORN Prayer Journal

FOR QUICK
PRAYERS, PRAISE,
AND THANKS

BARRY ADAMS

ROCKRIDGE
PRESS

For general information on our other products and services or to obtain technical support, please contact our Customer Care Department within the United States at (866) 744-2665, or outside the United States at (510) 253-0500.

Rockridge Press publishes its books in a variety of electronic and print formats. Some content that appears in print may not be available in electronic books, and vice versa.

Interior and Cover Designer: Peatra Jariya
Art Producer: Samantha Ulban
Editor: Adrienne Ingrum, with John Makowski
Production Editor: Rachel Taenzler

All illustrations used under license © Aleksandra Nikitina/iStock. Author Photo courtesy of © Nick Mirka.

All Scripture quotations marked NIV are from THE HOLY BIBLE, NEW INTERNATIONAL VERSION®, NIV® Copyright © 1973, 1978, 2011 by Biblica, Inc.® Used by permission. All rights reserved worldwide.

Scripture quotations marked NKJV are from New King James Version®. Copyright © 1982 by Thomas Nelson. Used by permission. All rights reserved.

ISBN: Print 978-1-64611-467-2

R0

WHAT ARE POPCORN PRAYERS?

Popcorn prayers are those spontaneous, split-second promptings that happen when we make a connection with God. They are short conversations with the Almighty that can be as simple as crying out "Help!" in our time of need or "Thank you, Lord!" in a moment of celebration.

A popcorn prayer can be a petition, a shout of praise, a concern for a loved one, or any other outreach to God. Typically, these rapid-fire occurrences go unnoticed in our busy day. We may even dismiss them as unimportant fleeting thoughts. They may get lost in the whirlwind of our daily activities. Yet these simple longings of the heart are interwoven into our everyday lives and touch everything we hold dear. This journal is a tool to help you be mindful of them.

Each one of these prayers is important to God because no detail in our lives is insignificant in the sight of our Creator. Check out **Matthew 6:8**, where Jesus describes God's attentiveness.

This small prayer journal is a handy place to record these conversations when they come to mind and keep track of ways your prayers are answered. It will become a lasting reminder of God's faithfulness. When you need reassurance that your prayers are being heard, you can refer back to what you have written and be encouraged that the cries of your heart were answered again and again.

HOW WE PRAY

Prayer is the way we talk to God. It can be as intuitive as a sigh under our breath, or it can be a profound time of intense, prolonged intercession. There is no wrong way to pray, as long as we are communicating sincerely with our Lord. Here are a few types of prayers that may help you develop your own unique dialogue with God.

"Wow! It's all about You, God."

When we focus on the Lord's greatness, we gain an amazing perspective on life. In the immeasurable vastness of our Creator's eternal glory, even the greatest of our problems pale in comparison.

To **worship** is to focus awe on God. We can worship during church services, prayer meetings, and in our daily devotions. But **Romans 12:1** encourages us to present our entire lives as a living sacrifice, meaning we can experience the Almighty's magnificence in everything. Journal your prayers of worship, and the circumstances surrounding those prayers, to record your feelings about the lover of your soul.

"You mean so much to me, Lord."

Worship is about who God is. **Praise** is where worship becomes personal. When you are awestruck by what God has done or created, and it takes your breath away, you express it. Expression of your personal appreciation for God in your own, individual way is praise (**Psalm 150:2**). Journal your prayers of praise, and the situations where you say those prayers, to record your words and thoughts about your Lord.

"I'm sorry, Lord."

In every relationship, there are times when we need to make things right with those we love. The same is true in our relationship with the Almighty. Recording short prayers of **confession** is a wonderful way to keep accounts in our daily walk in the footsteps of Jesus. When we confess our shortcomings in an ongoing, open dialogue with God, we are loved and forgiven, and our wrongs are forgotten (**Hebrews 8:12** and **1 John 1:9**). Popcorn prayers of confession can be as simple as "I'm sorry, Lord, for being angry at . . ." or "Forgive me for not trusting You today." Jotting down those prayers creates a reminder not to repeat the same wrongs.

"_____ needs You, Lord God."

When we pray for others and ask for help on their behalf, we are interceding for them, praying intercessory prayers. A popcorn prayer of **intercession** might be that random thought about someone that leads you to utter a word to God. It might just be the Holy Spirit prompting you to stand in the gap in that very moment. When a friend or loved one is hurting or needs protection, be bold in asking the God of all Comfort for help. Then jot down that prayer of intercession; it might turn out to later prove God was intervening.

Maybe the one you are interceding for is praying, too, but they need the support of another voice calling out. Or maybe they lack the confidence or the strength to pray like you do and simply cannot bear their burden alone. Whatever the circumstance, the next time a person's need comes to mind and you pray, know that God has invited you to share in the intercessory role of Jesus (**Romans 8:34**). However brief, that prayer is worth noting.

Our world needs intercessory prayer. We intercede not only for individuals, but also for entire groups and structures.

"Thank You, God!"

Prayers of **gratitude** happen when we focus on and celebrate the many things that God has done for us. Prayers of thanksgiving go beyond feeling grateful; they put our gratitude in words to the Giver of every good gift (**James 1:17**).

Thankfulness brings us joy and a deeper appreciation of God's goodness. When we wake up and spontaneously utter, "Thank you, God, for a new day!" or feel the warm sun, gentle breezes, or even brisk cold and thank God for creation, we are allowing thankfulness to permeate our lives as **1 Thessalonians 5:18** instructs: In everything give thanks, for this is the will of God in Christ Jesus for you. Jot down those quick prayers of thanksgiving; let this be your gratitude journal.

"Please" or "Would you . . . ?"

God is practical and interested in every area of your life and wants you to make your requests known about everything that matters to you (**Philippians 4:6**). Prayers of **petition** are when we ask God for what we want or need (in both the physical and the spiritual realm) with the confident expectation that our Lord hears our prayers.

When you have a financial, health, safety, or other personal need and ask God to meet it, jot it down, knowing that whatever the need, the Lord is able to help (**Matthew 7:11**). Jotting it down also allows you to look back—often in wonder!— at how those prayers were answered.

"Help!"

The Bible says that, though we live here on planet Earth, there are other nonmaterial forces at work that we contend with. When we recognize this in everyday life and focus our utterances heavenward, those are prayers of **spiritual warfare**. **Ephesians 6:12** describes these struggles.

So when you face inexplicable hardships and struggles, be encouraged that God can help you rise above every circumstance when you pray and cast every care upon the One who cares for you (**1 Peter 5:7**). Record those prayers and page back to journal the outcomes later.

"You're with me, God."

Oftentimes when we think of **communion**, we think of the holy sacrament celebrated in church services. However, learning to commune with God at all times is probably the most important aspect of prayer life. **1 Thessalonians 5:17** (NIV) says we are to pray continually.

The only practical way to do this is to increase our awareness of the All-Sufficient One's closeness every moment of the day. Think of it this way: Do you have to focus on every breath you take? Of course not. In the same way, learning to abide in the ever-present nearness of God is communication. Communing with God is simply growing in your awareness of God's closeness at all times. When you close your eyes, take a deep breath, and become more aware that your Lord is with you right then and there, whatever words you utter or think are prayers of communion. They're too precious *not* to jot down.

"Bless me, Lord."

When we ask for God's favor or for God to affirm us, we are seeking a **blessing**. Humanity started with a blessing (**Genesis 1:28**) and through Christ we now have access to every spiritual blessing (**Ephesians 1:3**). So don't be afraid to ask for blessings, because God loves to bless us! Be bold in asking and mindful to record the blessings you seek and the ways God blesses you.

A Prayer Journal

A prayer life is foundational to a believer's relationship with God. It is how we keep in constant communication with our Lord, express our hopes and fears, and make our requests.

When we record our prayers in a journal, we create a permanent record of them and solidify our divine conversations. Prayers and answers written down also serve as a historical account of God's faithfulness to us and to others for years to come.

How many times have you been prompted by a thought or uttered a prayer, but because you didn't write it down, the impression was gone? The more we take quick opportunities to jot down our thoughts and prayers in the moment, the more open our hearts become to the reality that prayer *really* does change things.

Using a prayer journal can also be of great value to record notes and key Scriptures at church, Bible studies, training sessions, or conferences that you want to revisit later in prayer. It can be a tool to capture important details of every form of ministry that you are involved in, whether it is hospital visitation, missions, fellowship times, or prep for teaching. Having a dedicated place that you can refer back to during prayer time will become essential as you use it more and more. The gentle prompts included in this journal will help you to organize your thoughts, notes, and prayers with ease.

This journal can also be a place where you note the details of when you have asked others to pray for you. It can help build a greater sense of community and belonging, knowing that others are carrying you in their hearts just like you are carrying them.

In this digital age, we can be overwhelmed with screen time, and there's something reassuring and tactile about writing prayers down. No keyboard can replace your hand-writing, which is uniquely yours!

Incorporate journaling prayer as part of your daily lifestyle. It will refresh your prayer life and help your relationship with God flourish—and it will document how God has truly heard the longings of your heart!

POPCORN PRAYER IN SHORT

There is an old saying that if you don't aim for something, you definitely won't hit it. Prayer is like that. Be as **specific** as you can with your prayers and, where possible, have a measurable purpose (**Mark 11:24**).

Jesus in **Matthew 7:7** encourages persistence in our prayer life. **Keep at it.**

Just like breathing is intuitive to our human bodies, our inner being can be in a **continual** state of communion with God (**John 14:16 and 23**).

Don't be timid! **Hebrews 4:16** invites us to come **boldly** to the throne of our gracious God.

Pray with a believing heart (**Mark 11:24**).

WHY PERTINENT SCRIPTURES ARE IMPORTANT

The Bible is the Word of God. It has power beyond our comprehension. When we pray in agreement with what is in the Bible, we have assurance that we are praying according to God's will and divine purpose. That is why meaningful Scriptures about prayer are so helpful.

Romans 10:17 (NKJV) tells us that faith comes by hearing, and hearing by the Word of God. When we align our requests with God's Word, our faith is strengthened, and we have confidence that God hears us (**1 John 5:14-15**).

Here are some much loved passages about prayer to read in your own Bible:

Philippians 4:6
Matthew 7:7-11
1 Thessalonians 5:16-18
Matthew 6:5-8

GOD'S PROMISES

God is the ultimate promise keeper and loves it when you simply believe your prayers will be answered. We are told in **2 Corinthians 1:20** (NIV) that no matter how many promises God has made, they are answered "Yes" in Christ. So, whenever you read a promise in God's Word, the Bible, shout out a big "Yes and Amen!" When you pray, trust it to come to fruition in your life. **Proverbs 3:5-6** encourages us in this journey of trust.

Here are some much loved passages about God's promises to read in your own Bible:

Joshua 23:14
Romans 4:20-21
Psalm 37:4
Mark 11:24
Philippians 4:19

Write some of your favorite Scripture passages about God's promises below.

WAYS GOD ANSWERS PRAYERS

Every prayer breathed to God receives a response. God answers prayers in three essential ways: yes, no, and wait. In every circumstance, realize the Lord is close to you and intently listening to your every prayer (**Psalm 34:15**).

Sometimes the answer is an immediate "Yes." It is exciting when God answers this way. A "Yes" from God is incredibly satisfying. We want to shout out a big "Amen" (**1 John 5:14-15**).

Sometimes the Lord answers a decisive "No." No excitement. But a "No" answer can be as much an expression of God's care and concern as a "Yes." Just as a loving parent says "No" to requests from their child because they see the big picture of what a "Yes" might do, so, too, do we have to trust that Almighty God knows what will ultimately work for our good (**Romans 8:28**).

When we feel prayers are unanswered, perhaps God is actually saying, "Wait" or "Not now." It feels like God's response is an eternity of waiting, but God *has* replied. We live in the confines of human time, but God relates to us beyond time and knows what is best for us. God's perspective is eternity. A day is as a thousand years and a thousand years is as a day to God (**2 Peter 3:8**). Waiting for an answer might feel like a thousand years already, but be comforted that God is looking out for your best interests in the long haul. If you are in a season of waiting for an answer, know the promises to those who wait, including **Isaiah 40:31** and **Psalm 37:9**.

No matter where we are in the process of receiving answers to prayer, we should trust God's goodness and purpose (**Proverbs 19:21**).

Read these Scriptures in your own Bible to help you discern God's voice:

Proverbs 3:5-6
John 10:27-28

Today's defining moment

What's on my heart

Beautiful things about God

Today's Word for me

A significant event

....
....
....

Things I'm thankful for

Who God is to me

....
....
....
....

God's promise to me

....
....
....
....

Today's milestone

I'm asking God for

My praise report

A verse I'm claiming

A marker or memory

My greatest need

Things to celebrate

A Scripture for today

An answered prayer

People on my heart

Remembering God's goodness

God's Word to me

Something to celebrate

The longing of my heart

What I love about God

Today's key verse

Remembering prayers answered

What I'm asking for

I appreciate this about God

I believe this promise

An event to remember

What I'm believing for

People to bless

A verse to claim

Things that hurt

Who I'm praying for

Who God says I am

My answered prayers

Today's victory

What God said to me

My prayer for today

God's living Word

Today's defining moment

....

....

....

What's on my heart

....

....

....

....

....

Beautiful things about God

....

....

....

....

....

Today's Word for me

....

....

....

A significant event

Things I'm thankful for

Who God is to me

God's promise to me

DATE

Today's milestone

I'm asking God for

My praise report

A verse I'm claiming

26

A marker or memory

My greatest need

Things to celebrate

A Scripture for today

An answered prayer

People on my heart

Remembering God's goodness

God's Word to me

Something to celebrate

The longing of my heart

What I love about God

Today's key verse

Remembering prayers answered

What I'm asking for

I appreciate this about God

I believe this promise

An event to remember

What I'm believing for

People to bless

A verse to claim

Things that hurt

....

....

....

Who I'm praying for

....

....

....

....

Who God says I am

....

....

....

....

My answered prayers

....

....

....

Today's victory

....
....
....
....

What God said to me

....
....
....
....

My prayer for today

....
....
....
....

God's living Word

....
....
....
....

Today's defining moment

....
....
....
....

What's on my heart

....
....
....
....
....

Beautiful things about God

....
....
....
....
....

Today's Word for me

....
....
....
....

A significant event

....
....
....
....

Things I'm thankful for   Who God is to me

....
....
....
....

God's promise to me

....
....
....
....

Today's milestone

I'm asking God for

My praise report

A verse I'm claiming

A marker or memory

My greatest need

Things to celebrate

A Scripture for today

An answered prayer

....
....
....

People on my heart

....
....
....
....

Remembering God's goodness

....
....
....
....

God's Word to me

....
....
....
....

Something to celebrate

The longing of my heart

What I love about God

Today's key verse

Remembering prayers answered

What I'm asking for

I appreciate this about God

I believe this promise

An event to remember

What I'm believing for

People to bless

A verse to claim

Things that hurt

....

....

....

Who I'm praying for

....

....

....

....

Who God says I am

....

....

....

....

My answered prayers

....

....

....

Today's victory

....
....
....
....

What God said to me

....
....
....
....
....

My prayer for today

....
....
....
....
....

God's living Word

....
....
....
....

Today's defining moment

What's on my heart

Beautiful things about God

Today's Word for me

A significant event

....

....

....

Things I'm thankful for

Who God is to me

....

....

....

....

God's promise to me

....

....

....

....

Today's milestone

I'm asking God for

My praise report

A verse I'm claiming

A marker or memory

My greatest need

Things to celebrate

A Scripture for today

An answered prayer

People on my heart

Remembering God's goodness

God's Word to me

Something to celebrate

The longing of my heart

What I love about God

Today's key verse

Remembering prayers answered

What I'm asking for

I appreciate this about God

I believe this promise

An event to remember

What I'm believing for

People to bless

A verse to claim

Things that hurt

Who I'm praying for

Who God says I am

My answered prayers

Today's victory

What God said to me

My prayer for today

God's living Word

Today's defining moment

....

....

....

What's on my heart	Beautiful things about God
....	....
....	....
....	....
....	....

Today's Word for me

....

....

....

A significant event

....

....

....

Things I'm thankful for   Who God is to me

....

....

....

....

....

God's promise to me

....

....

....

....

Today's milestone

I'm asking God for

My praise report

A verse I'm claiming

A marker or memory

My greatest need

Things to celebrate

A Scripture for today

An answered prayer

....

....

....

People on my heart

....

....

....

....

....

Remembering God's goodness

....

....

....

....

....

God's Word to me

....

....

....

Something to celebrate

....

....

....

The longing of my heart

....

....

....

....

What I love about God

....

....

....

....

Today's key verse

....

....

....

....

Remembering prayers answered

What I'm asking for

I appreciate this about God

I believe this promise

An event to remember

What I'm believing for

People to bless

A verse to claim

Things that hurt

....

....

....

Who I'm praying for

....

....

....

....

Who God says I am

....

....

....

....

My answered prayers

....

....

....

Today's victory

....
....
....
....

What God said to me

....
....
....
....
....

My prayer for today

....
....
....
....
....

God's living Word

....
....
....
....

Today's defining moment

What's on my heart

Beautiful things about God

Today's Word for me

A significant event

Things I'm thankful for

Who God is to me

God's promise to me

Today's milestone

I'm asking God for

My praise report

A verse I'm claiming

A marker or memory

My greatest need

Things to celebrate

A Scripture for today

An answered prayer

People on my heart

Remembering God's goodness

God's Word to me

Something to celebrate

....
....
....
....

The longing of my heart

....
....
....
....

What I love about God

....
....
....
....

Today's key verse

....
....
....
....

Remembering prayers answered

What I'm asking for

I appreciate this about God

I believe this promise

An event to remember

What I'm believing for

People to bless

A verse to claim

Things that hurt

Who I'm praying for

Who God says I am

My answered prayers

Today's victory

....
....
....
....

What God said to me

....
....
....
....
....

My prayer for today

....
....
....
....
....

God's living Word

....
....
....
....

Today's defining moment

What's on my heart

Beautiful things about God

Today's Word for me

A significant event

....
....
....
....

Things I'm thankful for

....
....
....
....

Who God is to me

....
....
....
....

God's promise to me

....
....
....
....

Today's milestone

I'm asking God for

My praise report

A verse I'm claiming

A marker or memory

My greatest need

Things to celebrate

A Scripture for today

An answered prayer

....
....
....
....

People on my heart

....
....
....
....

Remembering God's goodness

....
....
....
....

God's Word to me

....
....
....
....

Something to celebrate

....

....

....

The longing of my heart

....

....

....

....

What I love about God

....

....

....

....

Today's key verse

....

....

....

....

Remembering prayers answered

What I'm asking for

I appreciate this about God

I believe this promise

An event to remember

What I'm believing for

People to bless

A verse to claim

Things that hurt

Who I'm praying for

Who God says I am

My answered prayers

Today's victory

....
....
....
....

What God said to me

....
....
....
....

My prayer for today

....
....
....
....

God's living Word

....
....
....
....

Today's defining moment

_____
_____
_____
_____

What's on my heart

_____
_____
_____
_____

Beautiful things about God

_____
_____
_____
_____

Today's Word for me

_____
_____
_____
_____

A significant event

....
....
....
....

Things I'm thankful for

Who God is to me

God's promise to me

Today's milestone

I'm asking God for

My praise report

A verse I'm claiming

DATE

A marker or memory

My greatest need

Things to celebrate

A Scripture for today

DATE

An answered prayer

People on my heart

Remembering God's goodness

God's Word to me

84

Something to celebrate

....
....
....

The longing of my heart

....
....
....
....
....

What I love about God

....
....
....
....
....

Today's key verse

....
....
....
....

Remembering prayers answered

What I'm asking for

I appreciate this about God

I believe this promise

An event to remember

What I'm believing for

People to bless

A verse to claim

Things that hurt

Who I'm praying for

Who God says I am

My answered prayers

Today's victory

....

....

....

....

What God said to me

....

....

....

....

My prayer for today

....

....

....

....

God's living Word

....

....

....

....

DATE

Today's defining moment

What's on my heart

Beautiful things about God

Today's Word for me

90

A significant event

....
....
....

Things I'm thankful for

....
....
....
....

Who God is to me

....
....
....
....

God's promise to me

....
....
....

Today's milestone

I'm asking God for

My praise report

A verse I'm claiming

A marker or memory

My greatest need

Things to celebrate

A Scripture for today

An answered prayer

People on my heart

Remembering God's goodness

God's Word to me

Something to celebrate

_____

_____

_____

The longing of my heart

_____

_____

_____

_____

What I love about God

_____

_____

_____

_____

Today's key verse

_____

_____

_____

_____

Remembering prayers answered

What I'm asking for

I appreciate this about God

I believe this promise

An event to remember

What I'm believing for

People to bless

A verse to claim

Things that hurt

....

....

....

Who I'm praying for

Who God says I am

....

....

....

....

My answered prayers

....

....

....

Today's victory

What God said to me

My prayer for today

God's living Word

Today's defining moment

What's on my heart

Beautiful things about God

Today's Word for me

A significant event

....

....

....

Things I'm thankful for

Who God is to me

....

....

....

....

....

....

....

....

God's promise to me

....

....

....

....

Today's milestone

I'm asking God for

My praise report

A verse I'm claiming

A marker or memory

My greatest need

Things to celebrate

A Scripture for today

An answered prayer

People on my heart

Remembering God's goodness

God's Word to me

Something to celebrate

The longing of my heart

What I love about God

Today's key verse

DATE

Remembering prayers answered

What I'm asking for

I appreciate this about God

I believe this promise

106

An event to remember

What I'm believing for

People to bless

A verse to claim

Things that hurt

....

....

....

Who I'm praying for

....

....

....

....

Who God says I am

....

....

....

....

My answered prayers

....

....

....

....

Today's victory

....
....
....
....

What God said to me

....
....
....
....
....

My prayer for today

....
....
....
....
....

God's living Word

....
....
....
....

Today's defining moment

....
....
....
....

What's on my heart

....
....
....
....
....

Beautiful things about God

....
....
....
....
....

Today's Word for me

....
....
....
....

A significant event

....

....

....

....

Things I'm thankful for

....

....

....

....

Who God is to me

....

....

....

....

God's promise to me

....

....

....

....

Today's milestone

I'm asking God for

My praise report

A verse I'm claiming

A marker or memory

My greatest need

Things to celebrate

A Scripture for today

An answered prayer

....
....
....

People on my heart

....
....
....
....

Remembering God's goodness

....
....
....
....

God's Word to me

....
....
....
....

Something to celebrate

The longing of my heart

What I love about God

Today's key verse

Remembering prayers answered

What I'm asking for

I appreciate this about God

I believe this promise

An event to remember

What I'm believing for

People to bless

A verse to claim

Things that hurt

....

....

....

Who I'm praying for

....

....

....

....

Who God says I am

....

....

....

....

My answered prayers

....

....

....

....

Today's victory

What God said to me

My prayer for today

God's living Word

Today's defining moment

What's on my heart

Beautiful things about God

Today's Word for me

DATE

A significant event

....

....

....

Things I'm thankful for   Who God is to me

....

....

....

....

God's promise to me

....

....

....

....

Today's milestone

I'm asking God for

My praise report

A verse I'm claiming

A marker or memory

My greatest need

Things to celebrate

A Scripture for today

An answered prayer

People on my heart

Remembering God's goodness

God's Word to me

Something to celebrate

The longing of my heart

What I love about God

Today's key verse

Remembering prayers answered

What I'm asking for

I appreciate this about God

I believe this promise

An event to remember

What I'm believing for

People to bless

A verse to claim

Things that hurt

....

....

....

Who I'm praying for

....

....

....

....

Who God says I am

....

....

....

....

My answered prayers

....

....

....

Today's victory

What God said to me

My prayer for today

God's living Word

Today's defining moment

What's on my heart

Beautiful things about God

Today's Word for me

A significant event

....
....
....
....

Things I'm thankful for

....
....
....
....
....

Who God is to me

....
....
....
....
....

God's promise to me

....
....
....
....

Today's milestone

I'm asking God for

My praise report

A verse I'm claiming

A marker or memory

My greatest need

Things to celebrate

A Scripture for today

An answered prayer

People on my heart

Remembering God's goodness

God's Word to me

Something to celebrate

....

....

....

....

The longing of my heart

....

....

....

....

What I love about God

....

....

....

....

Today's key verse

....

....

....

....

Remembering prayers answered

What I'm asking for

I appreciate this about God

I believe this promise

An event to remember

What I'm believing for

People to bless

A verse to claim

Things that hurt

....

....

....

Who I'm praying for   Who God says I am

....

....

....

....

My answered prayers

....

....

....

Today's victory

....

....

....

....

What God said to me

....

....

....

....

....

My prayer for today

....

....

....

....

....

God's living Word

....

....

....

....

Today's defining moment

....

....

....

....

What's on my heart

Beautiful things about God

....

....

....

....

....

Today's Word for me

....

....

....

DATE

A significant event

....
....
....

Things I'm thankful for   Who God is to me

....
....
....
....
....

God's promise to me

....
....
....
....

Today's milestone

I'm asking God for

My praise report

A verse I'm claiming

A marker or memory

My greatest need

Things to celebrate

A Scripture for today

An answered prayer

....
....
....

People on my heart

....
....
....
....

Remembering God's goodness

....
....
....
....

God's Word to me

....
....
....

Something to celebrate

The longing of my heart

What I love about God

Today's key verse

Remembering prayers answered

What I'm asking for

I appreciate this about God

I believe this promise